新年好　　# We Love Holidays　　新年好

CHINESE NEW YEAR

Saviour Pirotta

PowerKiDS
press.

New York

Saviour Pirotta is a highly experienced author, who has written many books for young children. He was born in Malta and is also a trained chef.

Published in 2008 by The Rosen Publishing Group, Inc.
29 East 21st Street, New York, NY 10010

First Edition

The publishers would like to thank the following for allowing us to reproduce their pictures in this book:

Alamy: 4, IPS; 6, A.Parada; 7, Oote Boe; 8, Beaconstox; 9, Jon Bower; 13, Photowood Inc; Kevin Foy, 16; 21, Ryan Ghail / Getty: 10, Don Smetzer, Stone; cover, 20, Billy Hustace, Stone / Corbis: 12, 17, 23, Keren Su; 14, Dave G. Houser; 15, Phil Schermeister; title page, 18, 19, Kevin Fleming; Wayland Picture Library: 5, 11.

Library of Congress Cataloging-in-Publication Data

Pirotta, Saviour.
  Chinese New Year / Saviour Pirotta.
     p. cm. -- (We love holidays)
  Includes index.
   ISBN - 13: 978-1-4042-3709-4 (lib. bdg.)
   ISBN - 10: 1-4042-3709-7 (lib. bdg.)
   1. Chinese New Year--Juvenile literature. 2. Chinese New Year--United States--Juvenile literature. 3. China--Social life and customs--Juvenile literature. I. Title.
   GT4905.P464 2007
   394.261--dc22

                                                    2006026795

Manufactured in China

Contents 新年好

Happy New Year

Gung Hei Fat Choi! That means Happy New Year in Chinese.

新年好

The plum ▶ blossom is a **symbol** of hope for the new year.

4

The Chinese New Year starts at the end of winter, in late January or early February. That's when new plants begin to appear in the garden, and leaves are getting ready to open on the trees.

Farmers all ▲ over China **plow** the earth, ready to **sow** their new crops.

新年好

Get ready for the party

Chinese New Year celebrations can last up to fifteen days. But there's a lot to do before people can start enjoying themselves.

The New ▶ Year is the perfect time for a haircut.

Houses are cleaned from top to bottom. People decorate their homes with fruit and beautiful flowers. They also have their hair cut and buy new clothes.

Oranges ▲ are bought for good luck. They are supposed to make you rich!

DID YOU KNOW?

Everyone prays to the Kitchen God. He will tell the Jade Emperor how good the family has been!

Good luck everyone!

People write short poems on red **banners** trimmed with gold. They hang the banners around the house to bring blessings and good luck.

8

Some families hang pictures of the **door gods** outside the front door. They believe the gods will guard the house against ghosts and bad luck.

新年好

Sometimes **incense** is burned, to remember relatives who have died. ◀

Goodbye old year

新年好

The celebrations start on New Year's Eve. All over the world, Chinese people turn on bright lights. Families get together to eat a special dinner.

It's time for a delicious feast. ▶

In the north of China, people enjoy **dumplings**. In Southern China they eat a delicious rice pudding.

11

Dumplings have tasty savory fillings.

Where's the monster?

All that banging should give the monster a headache! ▶

There's an old story in China about a horrible monster called Nian. He liked eating people up. To scare Nian away, the people started banging drums and **gongs**, and burning **bamboo** sticks.

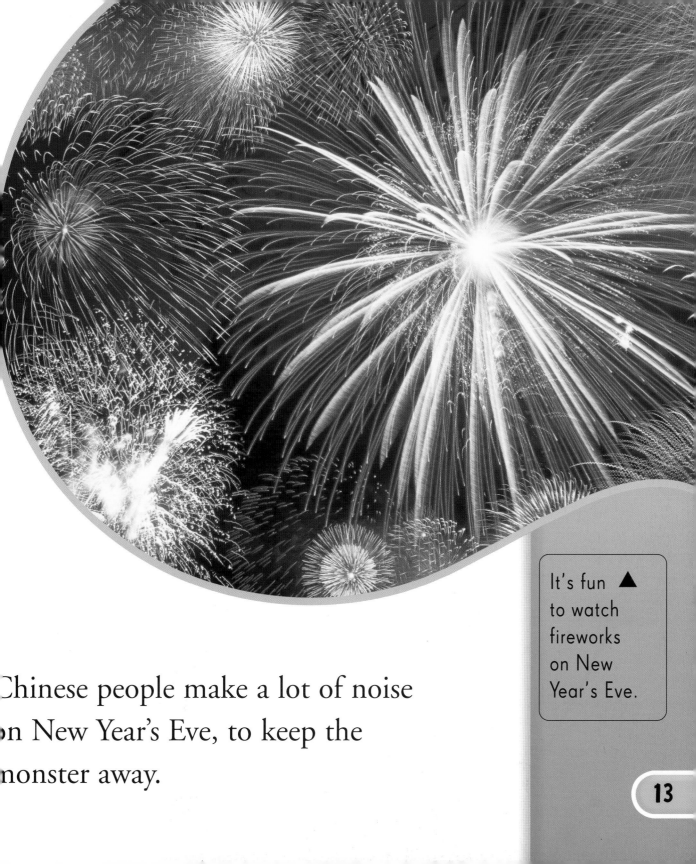

Chinese people make a lot of noise on New Year's Eve, to keep the monster away.

It's fun ▲ to watch fireworks on New Year's Eve.

13

Lucky packets

On New Year's Day, people put on their new clothes. They visit their friends and relatives to wish them a Happy New Year. Families offer visitors delicious snacks that bring good luck.

This tangerine tree has been decorated with lucky red bows. ▼

The envelopes are colored red for good luck. ▼

The grown-ups give children red envelopes with lucky symbols on them. The envelopes have money inside. It's the perfect New Year's gift.

新年好

Don't do it!

People are very careful on New Year's Day. No one sweeps the floor, in case they brus away all the good luck. Nobody uses scissors, in case they snip all the good luck away.

Nobody ▶ argues or scowls on New Year's Day.

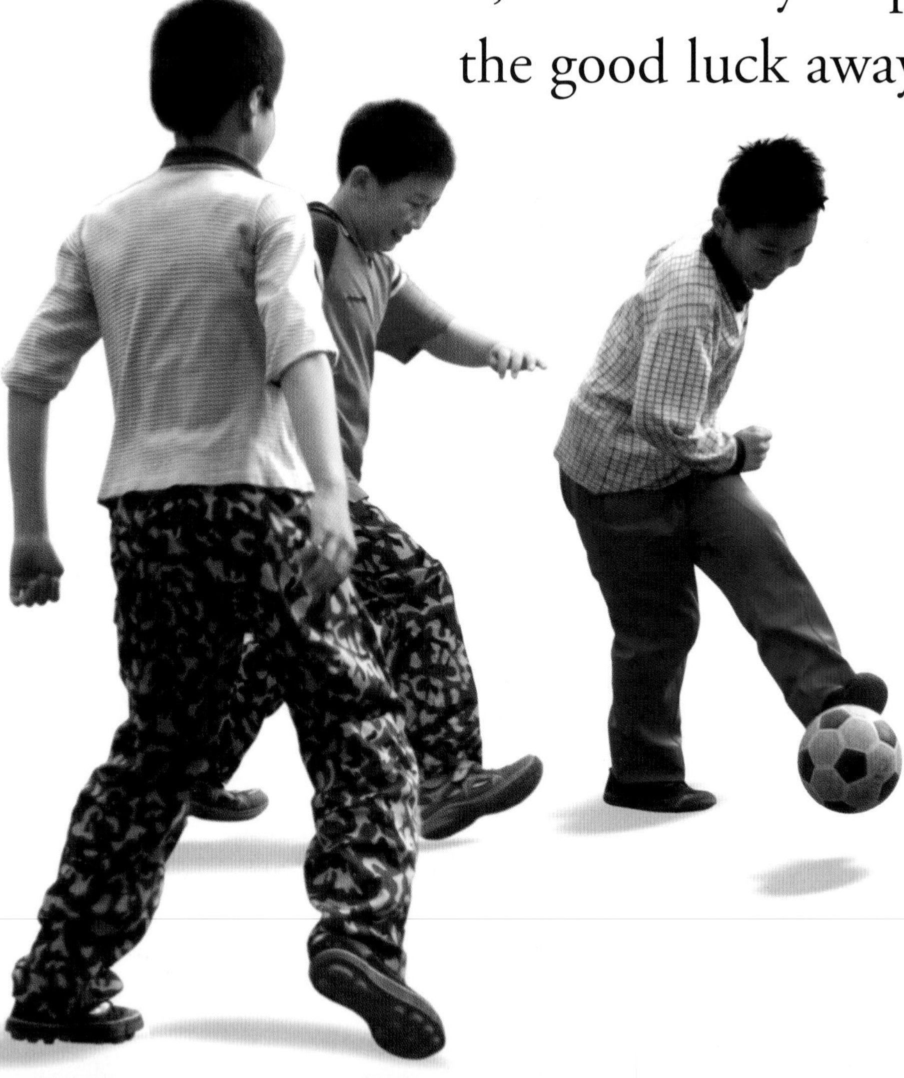

Everyone is very careful not to break anything. That would bring bad luck.

People put ▲ on operas to celebrate the New Year. Each part of China has its own style and story.

DID YOU KNOW?

On New Year's Day, people don't wash their hair, in case they flush their good luck down the drain!

Dance, dragon, dance

The longer the dragon, the more luck it will bring. ▼

During the New Year festival, many people come out to watch the famous **dragon** dance.

The dragon swoops and sways along the street. Its eyes blink, its ears wiggle, and its mouth trembles.

The Chinese believe that dragons are kind and helpful. They bring good luck!

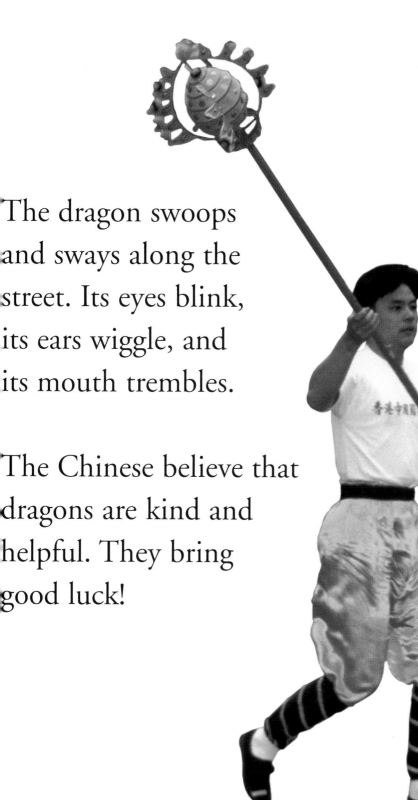

The dragon follows a leader, who carries a **lantern** on a long stick. ◀

19

Light your lantern

On the last day of the New Year's celebrations, people have a lantern festival. Paper lanterns are hung up everywhere. Children take part in a parade, carrying lanterns along the streets.

These children are dressed in red for the lantern parade. ▼

20

The beautiful lanterns glow in the dark.

What a wonderful ending to the New Year's celebrations. Let's do it all again next year.

The Chinese calendar

The years in the Chinese calendar are all named after animals. There are twelve animals in all. Find your birthday on our calendar and see what Chinese year you were born in.

Rabbit	1987	1999
Dragon	1988	2000
Snake	1989	2001
Horse	1990	2002
Ram	1991	2003
Monkey	1992	2004
Rooster	1993	2005
Dog	1994	2006
Boar	1995	2007
Rat	1996	2008
Ox	1997	2009
Tiger	1998	2010

Gung Hei Fat Choi!

Index

Glossary

bamboo a giant woody grass that grows in China

banner a large sign with writing, usually on cloth

door gods two fierce warriors, thought to frighten away evil spirits

dragon a mythical fire-breathing monster

dumplings boiled cases of food, made from suet, flour, and water

gong a metal disk that makes a note when hit

plow to loosen soil to get rid of weeds or prepare for planting

incense tree gum or spice that makes a sweet smell when burnt

lantern a lamp with a case around it to protect the flame

sow to plant seeds in the earth

symbol something that represents something else